I0756334

FINISHING LINE PRESS
www.finishinglinepress.com

# Poems for a Broken ~~Marriage~~ Man

*poems by*

**Leslie Archibald**

*Finishing Line Press*
Georgetown, Kentucky

# Poems for a Broken ~~Marriage~~ Man

ISBN 979-8-89990-393-9 First Edition


ACKNOWLEDGMENTS

Thank you to the following journals, where some of these pieces were published, for choosing to include these pieces and to give an emerging writer the chance to be heard:

Space in *Synkroniciti Magazine*, Space issue Vol 5, No 4
Fog, Born of Night, and Death on the Parkway in *Synkroniciti Magazine*, Haunting issue Vol 6, No 4.

I am so grateful to Finishing Line Press for acknowledging my work, guiding me through this process, and for supporting so many emerging writers through their contests and submissions calls.

Thank you to Writespace for providing a nurturing space for writers to grow and find their voice, especially Kendra Preston Leonard, Angélique Jamail, and Justin Jannise, who led the workshops where most of these poems were drafted, workshopped, and revised.

Thank you to the Houston writing community and to Holly Lyn Walrath, Elizabeth White Olsen, Ynes Freeman, and Jamie Portwood for your friendship, guidance, and support.

Thank you to my family, Mom, Kyli, and Lounes for sharing me with my writing and my writing family. A special thanks to Johnny, the love of my life, whose support, and patience allowed me to pick at my past wounds, heal, and move on from them.

Publisher: Leah Huete de Maines
Editor: Christen Kincaid
Cover Art: "The Wreckage of Stars," by Sana Shaw
Author Photo: Kyli Tabeche
Cover Design: Elizabeth Maines McCleavy

Order online: www.finishinglinepress.com
also available on amazon.com

Author inquiries and mail orders:
Finishing Line Press
PO Box 1626
Georgetown, Kentucky 40324
USA

# Contents

*These poems are dedicated to the spouses and partners who stayed too long in an abusive relationship because they didn't think they could leave, because they thought their partner could change, or because they knew their love would be enough.*

## Introduction

This collection of poems is an exorcism of sorts. An opportunity to acknowledge the effects an abusive relationship had on my psyche, my confidence, my security. This is putting it behind me and moving on, being the best version of myself, and saying goodbye to the scared insecure woman who stayed with a man for so many years because she believed he could change.

## Flying and Free

Riding on the back
of your motorcycle. Perched
with arms wrapped around
your steady waist. My head
rested on your strong back.
Eagles looking down on
a blurred world. Wind
beat against us. We
were so high I thought
we'd never fall. The heavy
chains we rattled held us down.

**It's Like Smoke**

Friday night lights
stealing a drag
behind the bleachers
watching boys
instead of the game.

Driving down the boulevard
windows down
radio up
cigarette in one hand
whiskey in the other.

Borrowing my sister's ID
to go to beer bust
or ladies' night
at a downtown club.
Staying for last call.

Waking up ashtray hair
hangover sheets
not being able to get up.
Wanting to be anywhere
else, anyone else.

Now it's like

Six a.m. you slip into bed
after being out all night,
my back is to you
pretending to be asleep.
I don't want you
to touch me.
I don't want to
fight. Trying to quit,
but I can't.

You won't.

I leave you
so I can breathe,
but I can't
because you are smoke
you linger and choke me still.

## A Pantoum for a Broken Man

I wonder when you became broken.
Did your parents love you too much?
They covered up your indiscretions so you
never learned how to distinguish right from wrong.

I loved you too much—but
not enough to keep you whole, or did I?
How do I distinguish, right?
I loved the person I thought you were

enough to know you were not "whole" at all.
Hiding in shadow—a remnant.
The person I thought you were
exists only in my expectations.

Broken, shadow man
hides his indiscretions and never learns. He
exists only as fragments of those expectations.
I wonder—when you broke me.

## You Are a Castle

Vine covered cinder
blocks sinking in heather
like poetry buried
in green and purple
moors. Your entrance
boasts of columns, your
greenery inviting
to passersby. They marvel
at your majesty not knowing
you are a prison full of ghosts
trapped in stone.

## I Never Asked for Roses

You'd pull the petals
from a flower to keep its
beauty for your own.

## I Once Had Wings

My mother gave me wings and told me I could fly.
She taught me that I had a voice
and that I could make my own choices. Then you

you held your hand over my mouth to silence me. You
picked feather by feather, pulled and ripped until my wings
broke loose. You held me down.
You told me I was nothing, I would never fly

on my own. I still heard her voice in my head
telling me I could leave    so    I
limped out the door hoisting my wings behind me.

## What if When You Said I Love You

What if when you said *I Love you* there were
  reasons to believe you, after six years
    of waiting for your family to matter.

What if they were not just words and they meant
  more than your addictions and you listened,
    and you got the help you need.

What if when I said *I love you*
  you believed it and put down that pipe
    long enough to remember and stopped trying

to hide your lies.

## Glass

Our love story is like glass. Not
the thick kind
like crystal bowls
that we might have gotten as a gift
for our fifteenth wedding
anniversary, you know,
the ones that might bounce a little
or roll and spin like a top only chipping
when you drop them.

It's like the glass they use
in movies. Sugar glass
I think they call it—the kind that
crumbles when a stunt man falls
through it. Rock candy
that melts when it's left
out in the rain.

## Space

There is a space inside us. Inside me. Where sorrow lives behind walls
built to keep me here. Home. Happy or seemingly happy. We fill
these spaces with dreams. We paint the walls and hang curtains and
pick china patterns because that's what our grandmothers did.
In these spaces forgiveness is no longer enough. Doors slam
and lock to keep them closed—to keep you out.

You force your way in filling this dream space with rage, with words
like slut and bitch and drunken fights. You smash the china
and tear down curtains one minute and the next disinterested
like a child tired of their new toy. You fill them with the worst
of you that knocks at night, knocks while we lie
back-to-back, knocks like the slowing heartbeat of a bad marriage.
You push and fill and push and fill until the door bursts open,
the room empties, and with nothing left, you lie alone.

## Earth and Stone

Earth skin molten burned and peeled layered
slick. Body rubbed raw, a djinn's lamp
misguided wishes. Beguiled by words I wanted.
No resistance. A stone falling. Addicted
to poison disguised as candy. Drunk
on dew or a light rain on our bodies in the grass. Who
tricked whom, got the last laugh before disappearing
into a blinding flare resembling the sun.

I jumped in not knowing where I end
and you begin, grasping at whatever looked like love,
a leap of faith into that light. I found
darkness pulling me under hot earth, a darkness
that hangs from your shadow and follows me now.

## Addiction

Derivative of ADDICT.
Formed over time
like a stone caught
in the current.
Resigned to the custody
of your high. To hand over
the self. Give in
to your next rush, living
to maintain the feeling.
You forget those you owe.

## Ashes and Dust

Your words surround me burning
like a California wildfire, me with no water
to douse the flames. I can only run.

A long dusty road stretches before me.
The cool night air extinguishes you
and your abuse. No "I'm sorry" this time.

A sandy dust fills my headlights and reminds me
of ashes and death and our marriage.
I stretch my hand out the window

spread my fingers and run them through
it, feeling each grain sting my skin
like the last time you touched me.

## Fog

Fog rolls in
from sea graves—
ghosts coming home.
Blinding billows swell
over me and I'm running
for shelter. Your voice calls

*come in from the cold.*
A whisper weighted by my
frenzied heartbeat.
Soup-filled lungs struggling.
Your laugh thunders over my
gasps.

I reach for the door
and hear you turning the lock.

## In a Desert Motel

Under bronze stars beside a shriveled cactus I
waited for someone to save me. Bug covered screens
ushered in cool night air and cigarette smoke
through a broken window from the room

next door. I inhaled the smoke like it was my last
cigarette and pushed my feet to the floor. The room
stopped spinning. Darkness settled. Colored lights

rolled across walls behind me. I steadied my stance. I knew
no one was coming. I knew

I had to save myself.

## Shrapnel

Words like pig and whore lodged in my brain
and burrowed deep within my skin

picked out with splintered fingernails
and left scattered at the door.

I stepped into darkness, closing the words inside.
I wrapped my wounds in pride and waited

for them to scab over. I did not look back,
I could not look back at a marriage like a bomb.

I wore my scars like armor and stood in the calm
of its demise. There was no blood on my hands.

**His Favorite Color is Gunmetal Gray**

You pull up beside my car. The moonlight
glistens on the gunmetal gray barrel
of your Glock. You didn't have to say
a word but you do. Come home you order.

You held on to me like the grip
of that gun. Leaving me
to wonder when it might go off.
When it would end. I knew

I wasn't going with you.
It started to feel like I could
pull the trigger myself
just to be done with it.

## Requiem for the End of a Marriage

A cadaver lies between us.
A stench permeates
our home. The walls
reek of decomposition.
We make no move
to resuscitate our life together.

There is nothing left for us
but to have the undertaker lay it to rest.

**Abandon**

*a·ban·don/ə'bandən/*

*verb*

1. cease to support or look after (someone); desert.
"A man abandons his family for addiction" (see addiction)

Similar: desert (your child)
leave (your wife)
turn one's back on (your family)
break (up) with (see break a heart)
(see jilt, strand, leave in a lurch, dump)
ditch (responsibility)

2. give up completely (a course of action, a practice, or a way of thinking).
"He had abandoned his ambitions to stay out all night and drink with his friends"
"She abandoned her marriage to save her child and herself"

Similar: renounce (your role as husband and father)
relinquish (the safety of your home)
forswear (lie to your wife)
disavow (your vows)
discard (your children)
wash one's hands of (the life you had planned)
give up (on your marriage)
(see drop, scrub, axe)
cease (supporting your family)
(see discontinue, break off, cut out, quit)

*noun*

1. complete lack of inhibition or restraint.
"He drinks with total abandon"

Similar: (see recklessness)
Lack of restraint (cannot stop drinking)
Lack of ambition (giving up)
(see wife leaves)

## On the Morning I Chose to Leave

Sun still hiding behind the dark of night,
your lies disguised as promises hanging
over you like balloons in comic strips
in my rear-view mirror. I look only

for a moment at your lips "Don't go" falls
from them. A last-ditch effort to maintain
control. Tear salted wounds begin to heal
while you grow smaller, eclipsed by a stone

shaped heart. I force my foot on the gas and
blaze, no wife, no mercy, no redemption
for you or for this marriage. Engine hums
blocking any inclination to turn

back. I cut the brakes to free myself—
no longer tangled in you.

## It Was Finally Over

You were laid with eyes closed
and crooked lips gushing gray relief
peering from a half-closed casket I
was forced to choose because
your family could not agree on one.

We bought you a spray of red flowers with a sash
that said "To Dad" from your loving daughters
even though your oldest bailed on you like you
were inclined to do and you never really
took the "Dad" role seriously.

I bought you a charcoal-colored shirt
and a skinny "eighties" tie, silk, like
one you always wore when we were young—new
before we were damaged, because that's the way
I wanted to remember you.

## Born of Night

You made a deal with the devil
hunched in some back room over
a line of cocaine and a Lite beer.
A deal that when you died you could punish me
because I left you.

Now you stand over me,
Morpheus's shadow behind you dark
wings raised. You reach out seizing bits
of streetlight that trickle through
my window. In darkness, you whisper
in my ear. I close my eyes tightly,
clutch the covers over my head, but
night after night after night
your face haunts my dreams.

## Absolution

Death absolves the deceased
from the horrors they commit in life.
*He was such a good guy*
*He was always there for his friends*
No one ever says
*he tried to rape his wife*
that would be nonsense.
He attacks her on her birthday—
*What a gift:*
She left him months before,
but she lets him take her to dinner and
she goes into his house, and
she follows him into his room,
*so … it was her fault, right?*
He rips at her clothes and calls her
a whore while she resists. She screams. Slaps.
*stop stop stop!*
She screams so loudly that his father
pounds on the door.
*Stop your nonsense*
because it was nonsense after all, right?
She clutches her shirt together to cover
bare breasts, slipping out the doorway,
past the father looking down on her with his sad blue eyes,
out of the house
into her car.
She locks the doors. She sobs.
Later, he'll say it's nonsense
and maybe it is,
but that night, he saved her.

## I Saw Death on the Parkway

He walked along the easement, the heat of the day beating
down on his slick tattooed head. Black trench coat covering
his bulging biceps and back. Bare chested and a cigarette
cupped between his finger and thumb to shield its ember
from the wind. I thought he was looking to catch
an unsuspecting texter or the speeder who didn't see
the sedan pulling out of the 7- Eleven. Always there,

always willing to lead the unaware from this world.
I pulled around to get a closer look, maybe offer him
a ride. I wanted to touch him—to see if he was real.
He turned looking back. My eyes caught his.
I shuddered suspended in a stare,
his stare, that looked so much like yours.

## Self Portrait as Shattered

I picked up the pieces
of me you left behind.
I tried forcing them back
into spaces where they used
to fit. I trimmed the edges.
I threw the damaged ones out.
Some, I put on a shelf to look at
in case I needed a reminder
of the person I never wanted to
become again.

## The Sun in 8mm

The sun came up for the first time
today. It flickered between
trees leaving shadows
dancing on the road before me
like an 8 mm projector turning
my windshield into a theater playing
a movie of the long path ahead of me.
Looking ahead, I found myself
excited again to see where I was going.

**Leslie Archibald**, a graduate of the University of Houston, writes poetry, flash fiction, and nonfiction in a tiny home office in Houston, Texas. When she is not writing, you may find her roaming the city photographing Houston's unique character, dabbling in watercolors, and exploring genre bending and multimedia literature. She was the board treasurer for Writespace, a Houston literary arts center, and currently works at a full-time office position while writing and editing part time. Leslie is a slush reader and nonfiction writer for Interstellar Flight Press. In addition to her award-winning flash piece "Sherry Baby" included in the special section of *Companion of the Ash* (Spider Road Press) released in December 2018, her work may be found in *Tales of Texas Vol 2, Synkroniciti Magazine Vol 5 No.4 and Vol 6 No.4, The Best of Interstellar Flight Magazine: Years 2, 3 and 4*, and online at *Interstellar Flight* press magazine. Her poem "She Dances in Indigo" was chosen for *Colorstory*2023.

Follow her on Instagram and threads at @Leslie.Archibald; Facebook and Bluesky at Leslie McCoy Archibald or visit her website at www.lesliearchibaldwriter.com.

www.ingramcontent.com/pod-product-compliance
Lightning Source LLC
LaVergne TN
LVHW090541110826
845146LV00003B/1209

* 9 7 9 8 8 9 9 9 0 3 9 3 9 *